Policy and Information

in Juvenile Justice Systems

A report of the Seminar held at Newcastle upon Tyne, July 1987.   Papers written by Bruce Britton, Barry Hope, Martin Knapp, Trevor Locke, Eileen Robertson, and Graham Sutton. Edited by Bruce Britton, Barry Hope, Trevor Locke and Liz Wainman. Jointly published in Newcastle upon Tyne by NACRO and the Save the Children Fund.

Acknowledgements

The editors would like to extend their thanks to the following organisations and individuals for their contributon to the seminar and this report:

Richard Waterhouse of the Local Government Training Board, for his presentation, 'Policy and Planning in Local Government'.

The Home Office Research and Planning Unit for their permission to reproduce the diagrams on pages 15 and 16 of this report.

Logotron for technical support and advice

Newcastle Computer Services Ltd., for the provision of computer equipment.

Foreword

The importance of developing sound policies, to provide a clear framework for practice and programme development cannot be overstated. It is particularly important in the field of juvenile justice, which involves many different agencies, each with its own particular focus and methods of working. The Save the Children Fund is actively committed to working across agency boundaries in order to stimulate debate and promote the development of improved policies and practice in the provision of services to children, young people and their families. Central to our beliefs is the importance of working in partnership with other agencies, and we are particularly pleased to produce this report jointly with NACRO, who have made and continue to make, such an important contribution to the juvenile justice debate.

The report represents a significant development in the work of Contract, our juvenile justice consultancy in the North East, and marks a growing awareness of the need for co-operative policies between agencies working within the juvenile justice system. It has been published through our Practice Development and Publications Unit, based at Hilltop in West Yorkshire. This unit works in partnership with other agencies to provide an opportunity for the critical development of experimental and innovative work in juvenile justice, child care and related fields.

I would like to thank the authors of the papers contained in this report for their invaluable contribution to the seminar, and their subsequent permission to publish the work they presented at that seminar. It is a measure of the importance of that contribution that we are now publishing this report, and without their co-operation and help, this would not have been possible.

Oriole Goldsmith
UK Director,
Save the Children Fund.

I am very glad to add my comments to a publication on such an important subject, especially since these papers stem from a joint venture with the Save the Children Fund. We greatly value our links with SCF, which are particularly close in the North East, where, in July 1987, NACRO's Juvenile Crime Section and SCF 'Contract' organised the seminar from which these papers are drawn.

All of us involved in juvenile justice are striving for change, but we cannot bring about change without information. However, information alone achieves nothing; it must be shared, discussed and translated into creative, effective policy at both agency and inter-agency level.

The encouraging evidence of recent achievements in juvenile justice suggests that the importance of policy and information is increasingly understood. I am confident that this collection of papers will spread the message still further and make a useful contribution to the continuing discussion on this important issue.

Vivien Stern
Director,
NACRO.

Contents

Introduction

One of the most crucial ideas to emerge from our growing understanding of juvenile justice is the key role of systems management. An essential means of managing a system is through policy development. This, in turn, demands a detailed understanding of how the system operates. Such understanding can only arise from a detailed information base.

No-one who attended the two day seminar in Newcastle upon Tyne in July 1987 on 'Policy and Information in Juvenile Justice Systems' could fail to recognise these simple but important messages.

The seminar was jointly organised by NACRO's Juvenile Crime Section and the Save the Children Fund's consultancy project 'Contract'. The purpose of this joint venture was to stimulate debate among senior managers and researchers who have responsibility for the formulation of juvenile justice policy. The seminar focussed on two issues: methods of policy formulation and the relationship between information and policy. The use of models in policy formulation featured prominently.

Policy makers and managers concerned with criminal justice have much to learn from related disciplines and from the experience of colleagues overseas. To this end, speakers at the seminar were drawn from backgrounds beyond those more conventionally associated with this area of work. They drew on experiences from fields as diverse as aircraft design and econometrics and referred to the criminal justice strategies currently being developed in the United States.

The papers in this report represent a novel and challenging contribution to the application of systems thinking to juvenile justice.

Policy, Information and Monitoring in Juvenile Crime and Justice.

Trevor Locke is a Development Officer with NACRO's Juvenile Crime Section. Previously, he worked in NACRO's Juvenile Offenders Team which was responsible for providing monitoring and consultancy services to the DHSS initiative to develop intensive projects under the provisions of the circular, LAC (83(3)). Before joining NACRO, he worked in the Youth Social Work Unit of the National Youth Bureau. In this keynote speech to the seminar, he examines the role of policy and planning in the provision of services within the juvenile justice system. Drawing upon sources from wider disciplines, and from juvenile justice planning carried out in the United States, he proposes a framework for the planning process, and the formulation of clear, rational policies, built around explicit aims and supported by sound information systems.

Policy is an essential function of management

Policy is an essential function of management; without policy there can be no effective co-ordination. With policy, there is a sure and effective foundation to planning and operation. Both policy makers and planners require information. The way that policy, planning and information can be linked together is through the use of models.

The substance of policy (what we might call policy issues), the real meat of the matter, is important; of equal importance is the process of formulating policy. At every stage of the process of policy formulation there is a need for information. But what information is needed? How is that information to be used? What does that information mean to those who use it?

These questions are answered by modelling—modelling the system of juvenile justice, modelling operational systems, modelling policy issues. Our task is not to understand that policy is important, but why it is important. Policy is important to organisation. Policy can only be effective if it has been properly formulated, if it is well documented and if it is comprehensive. If we are to succeed in effectively managing the problem of juvenile offending, then we must be effectively organised.

We can only achieve an effectively organised response to juvenile offending if we have effective policies and if the implementation of those policies is effectively planned.

If policy is pivotal to organisation, then information is pivotal to policy. In order to obtain reliable information, we must design good systems of monitoring. We can only design good systems of monitoring if we have well-constructed and reliable models.

Concepts, problems and solutions

Concepts: Policy

Policy is a very widespread concept, occurring in a wide diversity of disciplines. One of the clearest statements of policy formulation I have found was in a book on the planning of local bus services. There is a vast wealth of thinking and experience on policy and planning but it will not be found on the shelves labelled 'criminology' or 'criminal justice', not in this country at any rate. Many of the ideas I have found valuable on this subject have come from the United States.

Rather than trying to define policy let us think about what it does: a policy creates a framework for rational and consistent decision-making and allows a multiplicity of decision-makers to decide in a way which is consistent, because they are making those decisions by referring to a common set of values, aims, principles and guidelines. Policy creates a framework for rational and coherent planning. Planning is a way of getting organised: both in the short, medium and long terms. Effective planning reduces disorganisation and dissipation of scarce resources.

One useful description of policy comes from the book about planning in business by the American authors LeBreton and Henning: they wrote,

> *'Policies are standing plans. Policies are general guides to future decision-making that are intended to shape those decisions so as to maximise their contribution to the goals of the enterprise. Policies are instruments by which goals are achieved.'* [1]

This leads us to the concept of the *goal seeking system*. Policy analysis begins with the current situation that we are seeking to change, or the problems we are seeking to solve. The system of policy, planning, operation and service delivery should seek to achieve these goals and should be driven by them. In the model of policy formulation I am advocating here, there is a heavy emphasis on goal setting and the coherence between goals and planning.

Concepts: Planning

Can we plan the criminal justice system? To what extent is it possible in this country to engage in criminal justice planning? Who is responsible for criminal justice planning?

In this country we do not have, at the local level at least, a Department of Criminal Justice. No overall authority, at the local level, is responsible for policy and planning in responding to crime. Ours is a fragmented system. The Police, Social Services, Probation, the Crown Prosecution Service, the Courts and the Prison system are all independent agencies. But within the system as a whole they operate in a way which is interdependent. In order to tackle the complex problem of managing crime, each of these agencies needs to operate collectively to achieve an effective strategy, but must do so in the absence of any official policy and planning structure, save that which is conferred through legislation and central government policy.

In order to achieve any form of strategic planning, all of these agencies must (to some degree) co-operate on a more or less voluntary basis. They must create any strategic approach to their common aims through relatively informal procedures.

Concepts: Strategy

The term *strategy* has now become widely used in juvenile justice but it is a term which is seldom defined. Often it is used synonymously with the terms *policy* and *planning*. A strategy is about direction, the thrust and direction of policy, planning and operation. It is both the route to be taken and the chosen means of 'transport'. A strategy is what brings together policy, planning and operation into a coherent system.

Concepts: Research and monitoring

Research and *monitoring* are terms which are often confused; they have quite different functions. I would characterise *research* as being a method of inquiry. Research is concerned with testing hypotheses, an investigative procedure conducted through the use of established methodologies and is usually time limited.

Monitoring is a function of management: is it the on-going, routine collection and utilisation of data as a part of control. Monitoring should not be confused with *evaluation* which is the interpretation of information.

Problems: Fragmentation

I hope that the importance of policy is not difficult to establish. But I think we must acknowledge the problems faced by policy makers and those who would plan responses to crime and the management of justice.

The first problem is that the system is fragmented. Apart from the official agencies of criminal justice, there are a range of interest groups, including the community, professional bodies, political parties and the media. Actions taken in one part of the system will often have repercussions in other parts. If such actions are not co-ordinated they can easily counteract each other. The need for co-ordination in juvenile justice is well rehearsed; it is this very fragmentation which requires a collaborative approach to policy and planning.

It can be argued that there are positive aspects of this fragmentation. A totally unified system of criminal justice might present society with an oppressive bureaucracy, a sinister centrally controlled arm of the state with rights of access into every corner of our lives.

Problems: Lack of impact

Juvenile justice policy has a long history of failure. Despite several reforming Acts of Parliament, little impact has been made on juvenile crime by legislators. In some cases, such as the Children and Young Person's Act of 1969, key components were passed but never implemented. Some of the responses that have been made to juvenile crime have resulted in unintended consequences, due to lack of foresight on the part of those who pursued them. If we are to increase the effectiveness of our responses to crime, we must improve on policy, planning and management.

Problems: Disorganisation

This lack of impact on the problem of juvenile crime is due also to disorganisation. Policy and planning have been weak and ineffective. Co-ordination and strategy have progressed only very slowly. The successful utilisation of research has equally been poor. The allocation and distribution of resources has been variable and patchy. Commitment from policy makers and politicians has been weak, despite the loudness of the law and order lobby.

Solutions

Against this backcloth of problems, what role is to be played by policy and planning? I want to offer three basic propositions:

- The quality of policy formulation must be improved; in particular, we must improve the structure and documentation of policy.
- We must improve the processes and infrastructure of planning.
- We must assume a corporate approach in all aspects of the task, laying corporate foundations particularly where policy is concerned.

Much more attention needs to be paid to goal formulation, particularly to the formulation of public and corporate goals. We need to make improvements to the writing and communication of policy documents. Training, as part of policy implementation, is an essential component of planning. Policy statements should offer clearer definitions of roles, responsibilities and boundaries of the agencies involved and of personnel within agencies. This will help to reduce conflict and to promote cohesion.

There must be an improvement in planning techniques and skills. Responsibility for planning must be located with an identified department or group. What we currently suffer from is that there is no clearly located responsibility for planning the justice system. Planning must be undertaken systematically. Planning infrastructures must be created on an inter-agency basis. We must develop corporate approaches and strategies.

Policy formulation

We need to pay very careful attention to the way in which policy is formulated. I want to offer a model of policy formulation in local government which has been adapted to the circumstances of juvenile crime and justice. The model assumes that we begin with an analysis of public opinion. It assumes that the statutory services are ultimately accountable to the public. Public opinion is, of course, very difficult to assess. It seldom offers us unanimity of view; there are deep divisions of opinion about fundamental

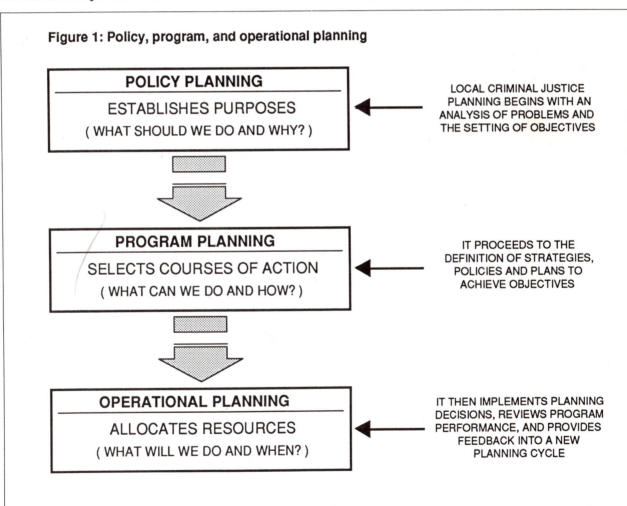

Figure 1: Policy, program, and operational planning

POLICY PLANNING
ESTABLISHES PURPOSES
(WHAT SHOULD WE DO AND WHY?)

LOCAL CRIMINAL JUSTICE PLANNING BEGINS WITH AN ANALYSIS OF PROBLEMS AND THE SETTING OF OBJECTIVES

PROGRAM PLANNING
SELECTS COURSES OF ACTION
(WHAT CAN WE DO AND HOW?)

IT PROCEEDS TO THE DEFINITION OF STRATEGIES, POLICIES AND PLANS TO ACHIEVE OBJECTIVES

OPERATIONAL PLANNING
ALLOCATES RESOURCES
(WHAT WILL WE DO AND WHEN?)

IT THEN IMPLEMENTS PLANNING DECISIONS, REVIEWS PROGRAM PERFORMANCE, AND PROVIDES FEEDBACK INTO A NEW PLANNING CYCLE

Source: Bert Nanus, "A General Model for Criminal Justice Planning", Journal of Criminal Justice, vol 2 (1974), pp 345-356

criminal justice issues. Public opinion is largely organised into political and particularly into party political processes. It is of course a matter of judgement as to how much political parties reflect public opinion. But they do provide very substantial inputs into policy systems, at both national and local levels. Both public opinion generally and party political opinion in particular, are themselves subject to a variety of pressures and influences. Issues of crime and justice, as well as concerns about how we should deal with children and youth, are issues which are open to widespread debate.

There are many sources of such pressures: professional bodies, national organisations, pressure groups, the media and so on; all contributing to the process of moulding and shaping the pressures which affect policy formulation.

The arena of public policy is, however, an important one for local government in general and for the criminal justice system in particular. It is therefore curious that the public policy arena, in our field, has been widely neglected. Very few of the policy statements which I have studied, have clearly stated what public policy is believed to be. There are only tangential references to what the public expect of the police or the courts. Gregory Falkin of the United States Department of Justice, from which much of my thinking has been derived, has put it like this:

> *The main input into the criminal justice system is public policy. Public policy may be thought of in this regard as guidance for the operation of the criminal justice system. This guidance may be in the form of priorities for allocating scarce resources and rules which place constraints on the system's behaviour.'[2]*

If we have succeeded in formulating a public policy, then we have a solid foundation on which to build the next phase of the process—and that is corporate policy.

Corporate policy on juvenile crime and justice is rare. There are few local areas which have, to my knowledge, formulated a comprehensive, corporately agreed policy. In this model, however, as presented here, corporate policy is one of three phases of policy formulation. It flows logically from public policy and provides foundations on which each of the constituent agencies can build their own, individual policies. It might not be feasible for all of the agencies in a local system to agree a detailed policy on all aspects of juvenile crime and justice. In this model, corporate policy should fulfil three main functions:

- Firstly, it should express those goals which are shared in common by all the main agencies concerned with responding to the problem of juvenile offending.

- Secondly, it should express agreement on the boundaries between each of the agencies involved. Such boundary setting should aim to reduce conflicts over which agency is responsible for what and what is the role of each of the agencies in the system.

- Thirdly, corporate policy should provide the basis for resource allocation, provide a basis for long term strategic development and should facilitate the workings of jointly operative systems, particularly those concerned with information sharing and cross-referral of clients.

It is now increasingly acknowledged that a collective strategy is required in order to address the problems

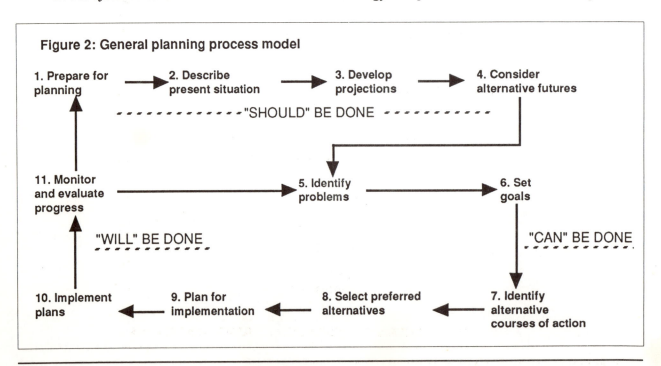

Figure 2: General planning process model

1. Prepare for planning → 2. Describe present situation → 3. Develop projections → 4. Consider alternative futures

- - - "SHOULD" BE DONE - - -

11. Monitor and evaluate progress → 5. Identify problems → 6. Set goals

"WILL" BE DONE   "CAN" BE DONE

10. Implement plans ← 9. Plan for implementation ← 8. Select preferred alternatives ← 7. Identify alternative courses of action

inherent in the fragmentation of the juvenile justice system and to increase the effectiveness of each of the agencies involved in that system at local level.

The third phase of policy formulation is that of agency policy. Each agency should formulate for itself a juvenile justice policy which flows from a corporate policy. How this policy is created is of some importance, particularly in terms of gaining commitment to it from those who will be responsible for its implementation. Some policy initiatives start at the bottom and are passed up the line for authorisation; in other instances, policy is formulated by senior managers and passed down the line. There are strengths and weaknesses in each of these approaches. Whatever the approach, the process by which a policy is to be formulated should be clearly thought through and planned. One key objective of the policy planner is to achieve a policy that is both workable and effective. At the end of the day an effective policy is one which presents a set of goals to which everyone is committed and for which there exists a thorough going plan which will assist in the implementation of the policy and ensure that the goals are achieved. Juvenile justice has, as yet, a long way to go in the development of effective policies.

A general approach to planning

The following brief description of a model of planning in criminal justice is drawn from Robert Cushman[3]. Firstly, let us look at an overview of the process (Figure 1). Three types of planning are outlined and for each a set of questions that orientate the nature of the exercise. This kind of process can be applied to whatever level of work we are engaged—whether public, corporate or intra-agency. The process is cyclical in that once the process has been worked through, after a period of time, it becomes necessary to review policy planning and re-work the other elements of the process in order to solve problems and improve on performance.

The same process can be considered in more detail (Figure 2). Here there are three elements to the process: what should be done, what can be done and what will be done. Between stages 5 and 11 there is a sub-cycle of problem solving. The process involves elements which are standard to policy analysis, par-

---

Figure 3: Structuring policy statements

Example:

GOALS	Aims	Long Term
	Objectives	Medium Term
	Targets	Short Term
DEFINITIONS	Tasks	
	Client Groups	
	Assumptions	
	Values	
PRINCIPLES	Of management	
	Of practice	
	Of systems	
BOUNDARIES	Agencies	
	Operation	
	Roles/Responsibilities	
REQUIREMENTS	Finance	
	Resources	
	Staff	
PRIORITIES		
STANDARDS		
ATTACHMENTS/APPENDICES		
	Codes of practice	
	Procedure manuals	
	Forms	

ticularly that of considering and evaluating alternative options and possibilities. The weight given to each phase of the process is of some importance, for, as Cushman points out:

> *'Today, some sort of planning process is regularly applied by many local governments and criminal justice agencies. Unfortunately, most spend a disproportionate amount of time and effort in operational planning, at the expense of policy and program planning. The need to respond to short-term workload crises, immediate political events, and a one year budget cycle tends to encourage a focus on operational planning and the allocation of resources.'[3]*

The central importance of monitoring and evaluation in this model will be apparent from its role in the illustration, but it is perhaps appropriate to say that without a full and effective method of finding out what is happening in the system, there is little chance to know whether plans are being successfully implemented or of identifying blockages and problems and dealing with them as they occur.

I would also highlight one other point that Cushman makes and that is that criminal justice planning should be comprehensive. What happens in one part of the system will have consequences, intended or otherwise, in other parts. Real impacts on crime and offending cannot be made by policing, sentencing or preventive measures alone but only by a strategically planned combination of all the elements which are available to manage the problem of crime.

Documenting policy

I end with a comment about policy documents. Policy is essentially written and policy statements are made to affect practice and procedure, that is, they are intended to be used. If we are to invest a considerable amount of time and effort in the production of policy (as indeed we should), then we must pay some attention to the way in which policy is documented. I do not wish to prescribe a standard format for policy statements (I doubt if such a thing could be produced which would satisfy all the possible requirements of policy expression). But in Figure 3, I offer some of the more common or more useful headings which might be employed in the construction of policy statements. The guiding principle in writing such statements is to do as you would be done by: write for the reader, making the document easy to use, easy to understand and above all clear in what is intended.

References:

[1] Preston P. LeBreton and Dale A. Henning: *Planning Theory*, Englewood Cliffs, N.J. Prentice Hall, 1961, quoted in Alfred J. Kahn, *Theory and Practice of Social Planning*, Russell Sage Foundation, 1969.

[2] Gregory P. Falkin: *Reducing Delinquency — A Strategic Planning Approach*, Lexington Books, 1979.

[3] Robert Cushman, *Criminal Justice Planning for Local Governments*, January 1980, US Department of Justice.

The Role of Economics in Juvenile Justice Policy Formulation

Dr. Martin Knapp is Deputy Director of the Personal Social Services Research Unit at the University of Kent. He heads the PSSRU Care in the Community Team and has worked for a number of years on evaluation studies, particularly focussed on costings. He is engaged in work on Intermediate Treatment and its alternatives, which forms part of the Cambridge-Canterbury collaborative evaluation of IT, funded by the DHSS. Eileen Robertson is Research Assistant in the PSSRU. She presented a seminar at the 'No Easy Option' conference held in Newcastle upon Tyne in May 1986.

This paper examines the role of a cost-effectiveness evaluation of juvenile justice services in policy planning. The difficulties and potential pitfalls in carrying out cost studies are outlined, encompassing 'hidden' costs, comparitive studies, the reliance on 'averages' and the relative effects of resources and non-resource factors on outcomes. Models of cost-related studies are provided, based on the authors' considerable experience of carrying out such research in the fields of juvenile and criminal justice.

It is no coincidence that economic evaluation and economic considerations entered the social care world during a period when resources became markedly constrained in public service provision. Economics has always been known as the 'dismal science' precisely because it is concerned with the scarcity of resources. Since resources are scarce the problem is one of allocating resources between competing uses and ends. Cost-benefit and cost-effectiveness analysis are two of the most commonly used tools which can help to inform resource allocation decisions.

These allocation decisions are already implicitly made, but various initiatives within local and central government have been designed to make those decisions more rigorous and explicit. This attempt has been spearheaded by the Audit Commission and its work with local authorities and the Financial Management Initiative within central government departments, both armed with the three E's (economy, efficiency and effectiveness). Policy and decision-makers are being encouraged to think about costs, cost-effectiveness and value for money. However, these issues are clouded by misinformation, incomplete information and gaps in understanding. The purpose of this paper is to attempt to steer a course through these difficult allocation decisions using economic evaluation in general, and cost-effectiveness analysis in particular. We will want specifically to highlight some of the difficulties and pitfalls which lurk in this area and find ways in ensuring that discussions of costs or cost-effectiveness are founded on complete and reliable information and not left floundering in a sea of misunderstanding and confusion.

Cost-effectiveness studies are one of the most popular forms of economic evaluation, but very often discussions of cost-effectiveness revolve around costs alone. The crucial aspect of cost-effectiveness analysis is that effectiveness features on the other side of the equation from costs. Effectiveness will be discussed in more detail later but let us first examine costs. What do we know about them? Discussions of costs tend to produce lists of average costs, sometimes comparing one authority with another and sometimes one form of treatment or disposal with another. Table 1 gives figures of this latter kind. These figures are readily available and are published regularly by NACRO who assemble them from various sources (NACRO, 1987). On the face of it these figures are quite useful—they are certainly the best available—but they hide as much as they reveal, particularly if we want to make use of cost information for policy development purposes. By examining the shortcomings of figures of this kind, we will also, hopefully, reveal some of the methods and approaches which economists would adopt in dealing with resource allocation in the field of juvenile offending. Our purpose here is not to provide a recipe for carrying out an economic evaluation but rather to give a flavour of the economic approach and how it differs from the bald financial approach. We will discuss in turn some of the problems of making use and sense of figures of this kind.

The first difficulty is that there is no such thing as the average client. Only the intermediate treatment costs attempt to give a range based on the intensity of the programme. For all services and disposals the cost will vary with individual characteristics and circumstances. The second problem is the false separation of services. It is rarely the case that one service or one disposal alone is received by any individual. In the case of juvenile offenders, a whole range of services could be received by any individual. For example, it is certainly not the case that custody precludes intermediate treatment. Neither does residential care preclude intermediate treatment. We need to view services as components of a 'package' of provision and not complete nor mutually exclusive entities in themselves.

Table1: Routinely available cost information

Disposal

Closed Youth Establishment (1985/6)	£267	per week
Open Youth Establishment (1985/6)	£320	per week
Probation Order (1984/5)	£730	per annum
Community Service Order (1984/5)	£640	per annum
Intermediate Treatment (1984/5)	£40 - £100	per week
(depending on intensity)		
Attendance Centre Order (1984/5)	£69	per order

source: NACRO (1987)

Third, transition costs are rarely dealt with in any cost figures. The importance of transition costs emerge particularly when there is any move from institutional to community-based provision. A shift of this kind is not a costless process. Resources which are tied up in institutions *cannot* be released very quickly. Large savings are realised only when a home or a prison establishment is closed completely. The rundown process and the very fact that resources are bound up in institutions create few incentives to change policy precisely because it is costly. A different but related aspect of transition cost is the phenomenon of increasing or decreasing returns to scale. As a service expands or retracts it may cost more or less per unit of output. It is therefore difficult to estimate the average cost of an expanded service on the basis of current average cost. The factors which contribute to economies of scale must be taken into account. Related in some ways to scale is the learning curve and the teething problems of a new service; it may require time to become less costly and fully viable. Time usually comes at a premium and this is itself may be an impediment to developing a new service or changing existing provision.

Notwithstanding these difficulties, average costs are generally relatively straightforward to obtain, but economic theory would suggest the relevance of the marginal cost concept in some contexts. In a situation of under-capacity the marginal cost of an additional placement in IT or a detention centre will be substantially less than the average cost. For other services or other circumstances the marginal cost may be very high, particularly those services which rely on a large input by social workers or probation officers. It is for this reason that funding a IT project on the basis of a per head average cost figure is not necessarily ideal. The appropriate figure to use depends largely on the question being asked.

When an average cost is quoted it invariably includes only the main agency provider. This is clearly insufficient since many other agencies will be involved in some way. For example juvenile offenders are likely to have contact with or receive services from the social services department, the probation service and the education department. The services or inputs which these agencies provide can be 'hidden' from view and community-based services tend to have a higher hidden cost component than institutional services. But even institutional services can include hidden costs. Consider a custodial sentence for a juvenile offender. From the time that the juvenile appears in court a number of agencies will be involved. A social enquiry report will be prepared by an officer from an agency; during the period in custody the supervising officer may visit the establishment, and visit and otherwise provide support to the family; social security payments may be made to the family to enable them to visit the youngster. Afterwards, during the licence period, a whole range of services may be provided. The cost of custody amounts to a great deal more than just prison department costs. The same is, of course, true of IT. All of the resource implications must be considered and not just the direct agency costs.

One feature of a service such as IT is that it is in some ways indivisible or exhibits 'joint supply' characteristics. This is common in the social care world and arises when it is difficult to identify and to separate

Table 2: Cost per unit of activity

	Groupwork	Courtwork		Casework	Individual work
Total cost (£)	36 932.34	36 427.25		48 735.15	15 828.15
Unit of measurement	Number of young person sessions	Number of cases in court with a report	Number of cases in court (no report)	Number of cases held	Number of young person sessions
	1 454	172	237	65	404
Cost per unit	£25.40	£186.14	£18.61	£749.77	£39.18

source: Robertson, Knapp, Crank and Wood (1986)

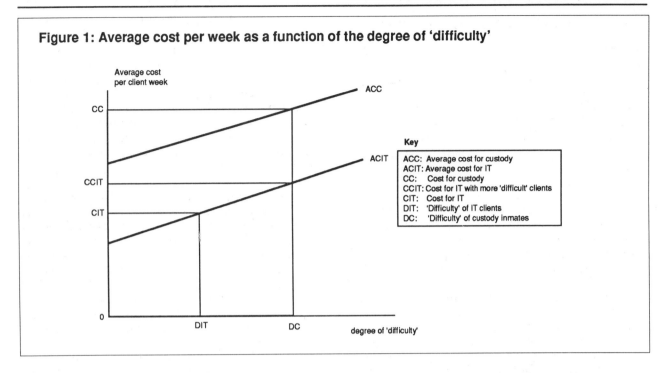

Figure 1: Average cost per week as a function of the degree of 'difficulty'

Key

ACC: Average cost for custody
ACIT: Average cost for IT
CC: Cost for custody
CCIT: Cost for IT with more 'difficult' clients
CIT: Cost for IT
DIT: 'Difficulty' of IT clients
DC: 'Difficulty' of custody inmates

out the services offered to each member of the client population. For example, who are the clients of an IT centre? The first group are those on IT or specified activity orders. The second group are those juveniles coming through the courts who may benefit from the work of IT officers' court work. The third group may be youngsters released from custody or youngsters attending for voluntary IT. Given these various groups of IT 'clients', it is clearly meaningless to calculate the average cost of an IT order to be total expenditure on IT divided by the number of juveniles on IT orders. Costings must take account of the whole range of services and functions which are undertaken under the banner of, say, intermediate treatment.

In a study carried out in Tameside Metropolitan Borough we attempted to do just that (Robertson *et al*, 1986). The methodology was unsophisticated but went further than other studies have done, particularly in dealing with this problem of indivisibility. In Tameside four IT functions were identified: groupwork, courtwork, casework and individual work. It was possible to divide up IT expenditure in relation to each of these functions, for example, the number of juvenile cases which passed through the courts and required a social enquiry report. The next stage was to define a unit of measurement which gave some indicator of the output of these functions. This allowed us to calculate, for example, that a court case which involves a social enquiry report cost £186.00 to the social services department. The other costs are given in Table 2. To cost an individual's IT package, or custody or other disposal, these various components can be added together. For a juvenile sent to custody, the cost to the social services department is at least the cost of a social enquiry report plus the cost of casework. This method gives a full

account of costs and who bears them. It is only by adopting methods of this kind that we can attempt to get around the problems of indivisibility.

We mentioned earlier the problem of undue reliance on averages. We do not talk of the 'average client' and we should not be content with average costs. There can be great variations around the average as Table 3 shows for prison establishments. Why is there such variation? What does it tell us about policy? Some recent work carried out by the PSSRU on cost variations between prison establishments explored these questions. This study examined all 114 establishments in England and Wales using cost and other data obtained from the Home Office for 1983-84. The main findings of this research were that cost variations were actually quite consistent—a high proportion of the observed variance could be explained by the set of 'explanatory' factors—and that the sources of the variation offered a variety of policy conclusions.

Table 3: Cost variations between selected prison establishments 1983-84

Establishment	Category	Average weekly net operating cost per inmate
Acklington	Category C	£ 184
Askham Grange	Female	£ 236
Buckley Hall	Closed Youth	£ 331
Durham	Local and Remand	£ 198
Frankland	Dispersal	£ 576
Leeds	Local and Remand	£ 150
Rudgate	Open	£ 128
Wakefield	Dispersal	£ 302

Source: Home Office (1985)

For example, large establishments—all other things being equal—are much less costly than smaller establishments. Second, overcrowding has two effects. In the long term, staffing levels are adjusted to cope with the high number and costs are lower on average than previously. In the short term, however, overtime has to be increased and the costs are therefore higher. Older prisons are *not* more expensive but multi-unit establishments are more expensive than single units. Not surprisingly dormitory accommodation was found to be cheap. Security category was a significant factor with Category A inmates being the most expensive and Category D the least. There was *limited* evidence to suggest that the concentration of Category A prisoners is cheaper than dispersal. Category B prisoners accommodated in Category A prisons are more expensive than they need be; that is, the mismatching of inmates and establishments is costly. Cost variations owe more to categories of inmates than type of establishment. Another interesting feature is that central London establishments have higher costs even after taking account of London weightings. These are preliminary conclusions that await detailed discussion with the Prison Department of the Home Office, but what this work highlights is that the cost of a prison sentence is dependent on the characteristics of the inmates. This offers one explanation for the ability of private prisons in the USA to operate more cheaply than public prisons. It is the types of prisoners which private prisons will take which allow them to keep their costs down (low security category, etc). For this reason, comparing like with like is absolutely vital. Any other compari-

sons can be dangerous. Therefore, when comparing the cost of custody with the cost of non-custodial disposals, again we must compare like with like in terms of the clients receiving each disposal.

Another crucial factor which generally fails to get through to policy makers is that any movement of one group, for example custodial cases into non-custodial disposals, will almost certainly push up the average cost of the non-custodial disposal. Figure 1 shows this effect. The line AC shows the average cost for intermediate treatment for different levels of client 'difficulty' or intensity. The line ACC shows the higher average cost for custody at each level of difficulty. If the average level of 'difficulty' is greater for custodial cases than the average level of 'difficulty' for IT cases then any movement of clients from custody to IT will push the average cost of IT beyond CIT. This problem of the rising average is one which is rarely recognised but could quickly lead to under-resourcing of services if constant average costs are assumed. The message is clear: local authorities and other providers must be prepared to devote sufficient resources to alternatives to custody which will allow for this potential increase in costs.

We now come full circle in our discussion of the omissions from available cost data to confront the neglect of output. Figure 2 shows how these components which we have discussed inter-link with one another. To make use of resources such as buildings, staff, vehicles and so on, expenditure is incurred at a level which is dependent on unit costs. Employing

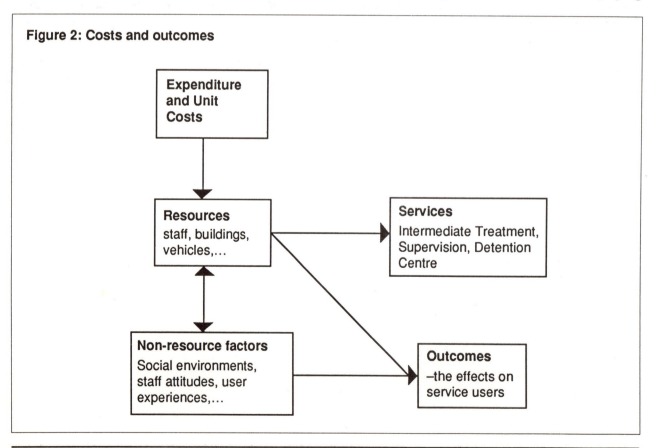

Figure 2: Costs and outcomes

these resources produces services. These services will produce outcomes, but outcomes are not just dependent on services but on a whole combination of other factors which we have labelled non-resource factors. These non-resource factors *can* be influenced by resources, for example, staff attitudes and behaviour can be influenced by staff training. But there are many factors over which we have no control but which will profoundly influence outcomes. In measuring effects, care must be taken to ensure that final outputs are being measured rather than intermediate outputs. The former are related to service provision itself. For example the number of places provided in an intermediate treatment centre is a measure of intermediate output whereas the impact on the individual of attending the IT centre represents final output. The sorts of outputs we would want to examine would depend on the objectives of the service itself. Final output measures could include; re-offence rates, the stability of the home family, school attendance, relationships with peers and family, and so on. This list alone demonstrates why it is that final outcome measurement can be difficult to operationalise. For this reason most auditing and performance measures tend to focus on intermediate outputs rather than final outputs. It is therefore important to be aware of the distinction and to see why intermediate output measures are a poor proxy for measuring final outputs.

If we can obtain all of the information in Figure 2 we would have clear directions for policy development and resource requirements and allocation. By having some of this information available, decision-making can be aided and informed. The availability of this information will also help to ensure that the resources which are required to fully finance and develop a service can be identified; and that financial blockages can be spotted and alleviated by the use of financial incentives. Incentive systems can be set up to encourage cost-effective use of resources, for example, one body which is responsible for all court disposals would respond to cost-effectiveness signals in a more consistent way than the present proliferation of service providers.

Even if detailed cost-effectiveness data is not available, we must be very wary of what information is presented and be able to recognise its failings and omissions. The ability to recognise what kind of information is necessary and helpful can only aid planning and decision-making in the field of juvenile justice management.

References

Home Office (1985) *Prison Department Financial Report 1983-84*, Home Office, London.

NACRO (1987) "The cost of penal measures", *NACRO Briefing*, NACRO, London, August.

Eileen Robertson, Martin Knapp, David Crank, Chris Wood (1986) *The Comparative Cost of Intermediate Treatment and its Alternatives in Tameside*. Discussion Paper 374/3, Personal Social Services Research Unit, University of Kent at Canterbury.

The Application of Dynamic Modelling Techniques to the Juvenile Justice System

Bruce Britton is Project Director of 'Contract', the juvenile justice consultancy and training unit administered by the Save the Children Fund. In this paper, he puts the case for a 'systems' approach to intervention in the juvenile justice system. By developing a 'model', he identifies key relationships within the system, and highlights the 'feedback structures' which underpin its 'goal-seeking' nature. Finally he proposes a role for such 'systems models' in the policy planning process. Barry Hope is a Training and Development Officer at 'Contract'. He concludes this paper with an example of a 'dynamic model' simulated on a microcomputer, using the latest modelling software.

I am sure that no-one these days can be in doubt about the *systemic* nature of juvenile justice:

- how a number of agencies link together to process young offenders;
- how the decisions made in one agency can affect the workings of another, ie that *interdependence* exists between agencies;
- how agencies pursue different goals some of which may be conflicting.

Nevertheless, various writers have claimed that the agencies involved in the processing of young offenders do not form a system at all. Indeed, juvenile justice is said to be a 'non-system' by some criminologist commentators because of the perceived lack of overall co-ordination and co-operation between the constituent criminal justice agencies.

I prefer to view this as a challenge to the application of the systems approach rather than an argument against its relevance. (In this sense juvenile justice is systemic but not systematic.)

Nevertheless, the 'non system' argument raises some important issues concerning the overall purpose of juvenile justice. A straw poll held among practitioners concerning the primary purpose of the juvenile justice system might well produce differing answers reflecting the agency perspectives of each participant. A request for each person to outline the broad objectives of each of the other constituent agencies in the juvenile justice system could easily bring wider differences in perspective to light.

It would not be unreasonable to conclude from this that there is no overall, mutually agreed, cross-agency goal which the system is trying to achieve. This means that, *as a system*, juvenile justice is not explicitly 'goal-seeking'. However, and this is crucial to an analysis of the system, although it may not *appear* to be goal-seeking it will still exhibit goal-seeking *behaviour* because this is the nature of dynamic systems. Furthermore, goal-seeking behaviour requires the existence of feedback structures. A feedback structure is a circular process in which departures from desired conditions stimulate actions to bring those conditions back to the desired state. The juvenile justice system is noteworthy for the crude and idiosyncratic nature of its feedback structures, largely due to the fact that its 'desired conditions' are so ill-defined.

A goal of systems management is to improve the system's goal-seeking behaviour by improving the definition of desired outcomes (or goals).

Our straw poll *would* have shown that the different agencies in the juvenile justice system each has its own set of goals. Some of these goals are explicit (eg. using community-based alternatives to reduce the juvenile custody population) whilst some, I suspect, remain hidden. Some agencies may have goals which involve influencing the discretionary decisions of others (eg court report recommendations aimed at influencing sentencing). Furthermore the goals of one agency may well conflict with the goals of another (eg. some magistrates may believe that the way to reduce the incidence of crime is to use exemplary custodial sentences whereas probation officers may argue in social inquiry reports against the use of custody, believing its use to be counterproductive in reducing crime).

In the juvenile justice system, such goal-conflict between the constituent agencies is the rule rather than the exception. Goal conflict arises at the overlap points between sub-systems or components of a system. Since the criminal justice system has many points of overlap between its constituent agencies (over eighty according to a 1984 study for the Home Office) the potential for conflict is considerable.[1]

One way of gauging the likelihood of conflict is to identify in which area of each agency's decision-making realm the overlap occurs.

If we imagine each agency having three main decision-making areas, their

- **duty** reflecting prescriptive legislation;
- **discretion** reflecting 'permissive' legislation;
  and
- **influence** which may reflect agency policy,

these may be represented as three concentric circles. The further out from the centre, the less authority the agency has for its actions (see Figure 1). When two agencies overlap in an area of decision-making, in general terms the greater their overlap, the greater the potential for conflict.

An example from the pages of 'Justice of the Peace' journal may make this clearer. It concerns the role of Probation in sentence outcomes. A duty of the Probation Service is the production of social inquiry reports for the courts when required. According to the Powers of Criminal Courts Act, 1973 these are to be prepared on offenders 'with a view to assisting the court in determining the most suitable method of dealing with his case'. In most cases the courts have discretion about making a request for a report except when considering the imposition of a custodial sentence. However, this particular debate was about whether court reports should include recommendations.[2]

Recommendations are a direct way that the Probation Service has of exerting influence on an area of the magistrates' decision-making. The perception of one 'Justice of the Peace' correspondent was that social inquiry report recommendations represented too deep an incursion into the magistrates' realm. I quote:

> *'Surely sentencing is a matter for the magistrate and not for the probation officer. The trend is sadly towards probation officers becoming more and more actively involved in sentencing. Indeed one wonders whether some probation officers would not rather be on the bench.'* [3]

The degree of overlap perceived by the clerk who wrote the above comments seems to suggest to him that probation discretion is reaching into the central core of the magistrates' responsibilities. Judging by the ensuing correspondence, there were a number of probation officers who felt that the reverse is true!

Goal conflict is not inherently damaging. It is an indication of parts of the system seeking different goals. The very process of conflict helps make those goals explicit. You can't have an argument unless you state your position! Effective systems management is about attempting to improve co-ordination between the constituent agents of a system. This is done by getting them to state their position in terms of an overall agreed goal. They will then hopefully act in opposition less frequently because they are more aware of the 'knock-on' effects of their own actions on other parts of the system, which in turn may undermine the likelihood of achieving their own goals. This, in essence is how the 'feedback mechanism' operates.

Given the complexity of juvenile justice, how is it possible to develop a clear view of how the system operates? How can we use this idea to clarify our understanding about a system which involves complex decisions made by numerous individuals working for different organisations and with different ends in mind? Moreover, how can we use this understanding to improve and co-ordinate the use of discretionary decision-making powers in order to achieve the desired outcomes and avoid the unintended consequences of our actions?

These are the types of question which form the 'bread and butter' of systems analysis and systems management. The purpose of systems *analysis* is to develop a clear picture of how a system operates and the degree to which it is achieving desired outcomes.

The starting point for carrying out this analysis lies in creating a simplified representation of the system which can develop our understanding of the elements and relationships within that system. In other words, developing a *model*.

If this sounds complex, it need not be, because each of us continuously uses models to understand and manipulate aspects of our lives. Most of the time, we are oblivious to the models we use because not only are they in our heads, but they are what we think *with* rather than what we think *about*. This paper is concerned with the importance of making our internal models about the juvenile justice system explicit—to ourselves and to others. This process is a crucial part of systems management and one which is easier than it may appear.

We can be helped here by the huge literature on systems analysis and model-building which emanates from the fields of operational research, management science, organisational development, systems engineering, and cybernetics. The techniques required for modelling even very sophisticated human systems are available now. Applications abound in hospital administration, ecomomic planning, telecommunications and many other fields.

Some modelling techniques have already been applied to the adult criminal justice system, as I shall

Figure 1: Duty, discretion and influence

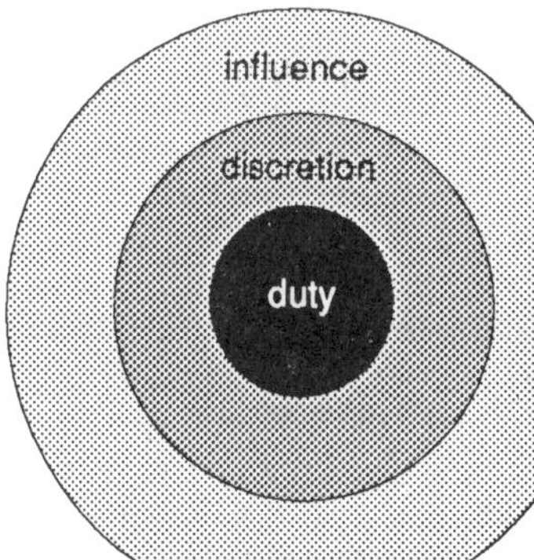

The decision-making areas—duty, discretion and influence can be represented as three concentric circles. The further out from the centre, the less authority the agency has for its actions.

explain later, and others have been used within its constitutuent agencies. Most still await widespread application in the juvenile justice field.

What is modelling?

Modelling is a process of building an abstract representation of real life which is made sufficiently explicit for one to be able to examine the assumptions embodied in it, to manipulate it, to experiment with it, and to draw inferences from it which can be applied to reality. In this way, models become a conceptual prop to our understanding which, although they don't convey the whole 'truth' about a system, do convey a comprehensible part of it.[4]

Models can be used in five major ways:

- to communicate facts about the system
- to communicate ideas about the system
- to generate new ideas for designing or operating the system
- to predict how the system will behave under different circumstances
  and
- to provide insights into why the system behaves as it does.

Building a model is a process which helps to clarify issues and relationships in a system. In this sense, the process of model-building is as valuable as the end result since it forces us to think about and explain the system we are studying and attempting to manage. As one writer has put it:

'I strongly suspect that the primary purpose of [system models] is achieved before they are completed. In the process of trying to sort out what is or is not important in a system, it often clears one's own mind to set things out diagrammatically. The danger is that you end up with a diagram which is crystal clear to you but like Hampton Court maze to anyone else.'

A good model, therefore, describes a system to its participants in such a way that:

firstly • they feel it makes sense of their experience of the system and its context.

secondly • they can ask questions of it and receive answers which are easily understood and interpreted.

thirdly • they can commit themselves to it as a framework upon which to co-ordinate their actions.

finally • when they do so they find the model useful and realistic so that their expectations of it are appropriate and they are unlikely to be surprised by unexpected outcomes arising from their actions.

Why should we develop models of the juvenile justice system?

All agencies in the criminal justice system make decisions which may involve changes in policy, practice or procedures and these decisions affect both people's lives and the use of resources in real and sometimes immediate ways.

Modelling a system allows us to take risks in exploring decision-making options without jeopardising real people, resources or reputations: to try things out in theory before committing ourselves in practice. In other words, we can ask questions of a model to get answers of the system it represents.

For example, no-one produces a prototype airliner straight from the drawing board and sends it up on its first flight with a cabinload of passengers. Such a complicated mechanical system as an aircraft has millions of pounds spent on it at the research and development stage. Scale models are built and wind-tunnel tested; full-size prototypes are constructed and tested to destruction in order to predict as accurately as possible how the aircraft will perform when it goes into commission with the airline companies. Even with this extensive modelling, failures still occur (like the Lockheed Starfighter or the Titanic) but these are the exception rather than the rule. Thankfully disasters are avoided largely as a result of the modelling process.

Modelling the juvenile justice system is, in many ways, more difficult than mechanical modelling. Unlike the propulsion system of an aircraft, the behaviour of a human system is very difficult to predict. This is because it is a 'soft' system which depends on the non-routine actions of many individuals rather than a 'hard' system where, for example, the tensile strengths of engine mounts or the thrust potential of propellor configurations can be accurately measured.

In a 'soft' system such as the juvenile justice system, operations and outcomes are largely probabilistic. In other words, within guidelines, decision-makers in the juvenile justice system may have a considerable degree of discretion about what action they take in certain circumstances eg the police have discretion about whether or not to caution an offender; the Crown Prosecution Service about whether or not to prosecute; a probation officer about what recommendation to make in a court report; and the courts about which sentence to impose.

The degree of discretion may be influenced by the Law or by agency policy. It is important to note here that the more limited the discretion in any decision, the more predictable the outcome and hence the more 'controllable' the system. Imagine how you would feel if, when the pilot moved the joystick of an aircraft, she could only tell you that there was a fifty percent probability that it would bank or climb. Would you fly in that aircraft with so little idea of what was going to happen next? The juvenile justice system appears to operate in a similar way most of the time.

Devising models of the juvenile justice system may be particularly helpful in understanding the way in which discretion is applied in one part of the system and the consequences this has for resources and workloads in other parts. It may also be used to evaluate decision-making options which do not achieve the desired outcomes or create unacceptable unintended consequences. These options can then be rejected prior to implementation—before any damage is done.

Models can, in this way, be used as tools to aid the management and planning of the system as a whole. More sophisticated models can be used to *simulate* and predict the effects of changes (whether planned as a result of policy implementation or imposed as a result of the system reacting to external events).

How should you go about building a model?

Modelling is a highly creative activity which progresses cyclically through a number of phases. Each cycle comprises five main stages and the model created using this process becomes increasingly complex at each stage. After each cycle of its development, the model should more and more accurately reflect real life. The stages involved in model-building are equivalent to adding a new dimension each time. They are, in turn:

firstly • clarifying why you want to build a model of a system and what behaviour you want to examine or represent.

secondly • defining the components and boundaries of the system (ie the **structure** of the system). This can be likened to drawing up a one-dimensional list. Venn diagrams are often used to clarify this.

thirdly • adding the connections, relationships, and flows between the system components (ie the **processes** of the system) involves depicting the system pictorially in two dimensions—the normal conventions for this are network diagrams and flow charts.

fourthly • including **information** to test the accuracy of the model in simulating the 'real' behaviour of the system adds a third dimension to the structure and process.

finally • **using** the model to test assumptions and system changes involves running it over time, the fourth dimension.

I shall go through each of these stages in more detail using the development of the Home Office criminal justice system model as a 'case study' of modelling.[5]

In 1979, the Home Office began work on building a computerised dynamic simulation model of the

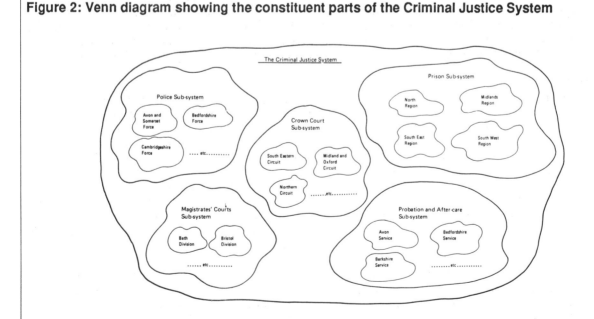

Figure 2: Venn diagram showing the constituent parts of the Criminal Justice System

The Criminal Justice System

Police Sub-system
Avon and Somerset Force
Bedfordshire Force
Cambridgeshire Force
..... etc..........

Crown Court Sub-system
South Eastern Circuit
Midland and Oxford Circuit
Northern Circuit
........etc...........

Prison Sub-system
North Region
Midlands Region
South East Region
South West Region

Magistrates' Courts Sub-system
Bath Division
Bristol Division
.... etc ....

Probation and After-care Sub-system
Avon Service
Bedfordshire Service
Berkshire Service
.... etc ....

Source: Home Office (1985). Note that this diagram was produced before the advent of the Crown Prosecution Service

criminal justice system (CJS) of England and Wales. The purpose of this was to produce a tool which could be used for the management and planning of the system as a whole. Its main objective is to represent in a systematic and quantitative manner, the principal interactions between the constituent parts so that the effects of changes in *one part* of the system could be demonstrated throughout the whole CJS.

It is crucial in a model of a system to be aware of who is defining the boundary. Drawing a boundary around the system is the way in which elements are either included in the system or placed in the system's environment. In Juvenile Justice, one agency's system element may be another agency's environment. In modelling the juvenile justice system, or any other system, it is crucial to include *all* the relevant elements within the system boundary. Since no one agency has an overview of the whole juvenile justice system, this is a powerful argument for representatives of *all* involved agencies being involved in the model-building process. Some very useful advice and techniques for building up models of systems can be found in the book 'Systems, Management and Change', produced by the Open University.[6]

Having defined the purpose of the model, the main elements of the adult CJS were identified by the Home Office researchers as the police, the courts, the Probation Service and the Prison Service. This is

portrayed in Figure 2 using a common convention called the Venn Diagram. A model of the juvenile justice system would of course, have to incorporate the Social Services Department, Education Department and, perhaps, voluntary agencies (Intermediate Treatment and Alternative to Care and Custody projects). Each of the agencies in Figure 2 were viewed by the Home Office as systems in their own right which represented *sub-systems* of the CJS as a whole. The inter-relationships are shown in Figure 3. As you can see, each of the sub-systems interacts with the others. Changes at one point have repercussions elsewhere and it is impossible to affect output at any one point without considering inputs elsewhere. At this stage, the model was a crude overall representation of the way in which offenders were processed by the CJS. In order to develop a more comprehensive understanding of the CJS each sub-system was modelled separately. These 'sub models' (including one to represent the flow of defendants between the other sub-models) were later fitted together to form the complete model of the CJS.[7]

Sub-models were created for the police, magistrates courts, Crown courts and the prisons. The probation sub-model is still to be devised. Each has been written up in separate Home Office reports.

One of the main factors taken into consideration by the Home Office in deciding which type of model to use was 'What questions would the model need to address?' These fell into two groups.

- Firstly, questions about the effects that specific types of changes would have on the workloads of the individual agencies that make up the system (eg. an increase in recorded crime rate or a change in policy influenced by a legal change).

- The second type of question was concerned with the effects of constraints on resources. The model would have to be able to assess the effects on performance that would arise from a constraint on resources while workloads remained the same.

The type of model which was devised is known as a *stock/flow* model. The CJS model created by the Home Office, therefore, incorporates not only the components of the CJS and their inter-relationships but it also deals with change over time.

To do this, the model was developed on a computer and was able to simulate the movement of defendants through the system over time. The model did this by manipulating very large amounts of information drawn from various sources using *rules* which had been extrapolated from earlier analyses. Building up this kind of dynamic model which allows us to view changes over time is a complex process which involved a considerable investment of Home Office resources.

Figure 3: Flow-chart of the criminal justice system

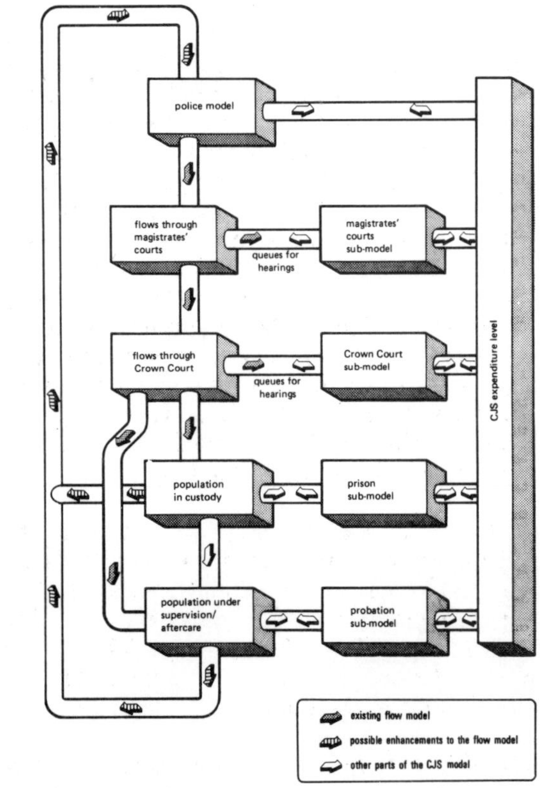

source: Home Office (1985)

The model which emerged was tested a number of times by running cases through its various paths in proportions that reflect actual practice. When this simulation was developed to a point which represented historical reality sufficiently accurately (tested by comparing simulated outcomes generated by the model from historical data against the actual outcomes) it could then be used for predictive purposes in a number of different ways.

For example, by using the aggregated information on trends from previous years, the Home Office CJS model would be able to calculate the probability of a male, aged 21 or over, convicted of robbery being given a prison sentence by the Crown court.

Or, by changing aspects of the simulated system and then running the model to observe the outcomes, the effect of decriminalising certain crimes can be measured.

Policy changes such as a transfer of resources from custody to non-custodial sentencing options such as probation could be simulated and the effects measured using the model.

These are ony a few examples of what is possible using the CJS model produced by the Home Office. In fact, a number of 'runs' of the model have already been made to investigate how the CJS would be affected by:

- Firstly, an increase in the persons prosecuted for offences.

- Secondly, the above run but with a decrease in the persons proceeded against for motoring offences.

- Thirdly, the second run plus a specified increase in magistrates' courts' resources.

The effects could be measured in terms of remand populations, Crown and magistrates courts, backlogs and a number of suggestions made concerning future areas for research. Those interested in more detail are referred to 'Managing Criminal Justice' edited by David Moxon.[8]

Despite their pioneering work, there are a number of major drawbacks to the Home Office model:

1. Its scale (covering England and Wales) restricts its use as a detailed planning tool on a local (say, County or petty sessional division level).

2. It runs on a mini-computer which needs a high degree of technical expertise to program and, at present, is only used in batch mode (where the user's input must be specified before the run begins rather than interrogative model where changes can be made during the run to investigate new ideas).

3. It is highly 'mathematical' and requires considerable computer resources. It also produces printout which takes a great deal of time to interpret.

4. Modifications to the model appear to be difficult to make.

5. It is based on questionable assumptions eg it states that the aim of post-sentence agencies (in this case, probation) are to 'implement the judgements of the courts'. One wonders about the role of probation in influencing sentencing?

6. It is incomplete:

   - it does not yet have an operational sub-model for probation
   - the model only simulates the adult criminal justice system
   - it only contains data up to the year 1980
   - it does not yet include recidivism as a feedback element

Notwithstanding these shortcomings, the Home Office model serves as a good example of the potential for computer modelling in the CJS.

Maintaining the model

It is important to remember that developing a model involves the continual refinement of its ability to simulate the behaviour of the real system. This means that the information requirements of the model must be regularly reviewed and the database of the model constantly updated. For example, projections based on recent trends are likely to be more accurate than those based on the trends of several years ago. Refining the model does not always mean collecting data about yet more aspects of the system. The purposes to which the model is put will, to a large extent, determine the information required to both 'set-up' and 'run' the model. A major aim of systems modelling is to represent in the model only what is necessary of the system to accurately simulate the system's behaviour. The most useful, and certainly the most elegant, models are usually the most simple. Returning to the aircraft analogy, you don't need a scale model pilot and flight deck in a model designed to investigate air-flow.

At this stage it is important to recognise that the practical value and maintenance of a juvenile justice system model will depend on effective dialogue between those who have responsibilty for initiating and formulating policy, those whose job it is to implement policies and those who monitor and research the effects of the policy.

Such a dialogue should take place across agency boundaries and concentrate on improving the understanding of the system's behaviour and how this could, in turn, improve the constituent agencies' ability to achieve both their own and any corporate goals.

How might a model of the juvenile justice system be used?

Figure 4 (itself modelling the systems management process) shows how a juvenile justice system dynamic model could become an integral part of policy development and implementation. Here, the model provides the link between information and practice. Potential solutions to problems could be simulated using the computer and the outcomes measured against goals to identify unintended and intended consequences, and 'knock-on' effects. Decisions could then be based on predicted outcomes, which themselves would be based on information about the system rather than on 'hunches'. The implementation of policy changes would then affect practice which would be monitored. The information arising from this could be used to modify and refine the model—and so on.

Given a model which covers the whole juvenile justice system in a locality, and access to information concerning all the constituent agencies, such a model could be used by any agency to test out alternative policy options.

A future scene might involve social services officers who, through an analysis of the monitoring data, have noticed that the numbers of young people assigned by the courts to an Alternative to Care and Custody project has dropped off even though the number of young people entering custody has shown no appreciable change.

The officers develop various ideas to explain this apparent anomaly in a brainstorming session. These might provoke the following questions:

- Has there been a change in the type of offending by young people?
- Has the gatekeeping 'dried up' referrals?
- Is the scheme losing credibility with the Courts?
- Is this a temporary anomaly?

Using up-to-date information in the model, some of these hypotheses are tested immediately using the office micro-computer. The results of these tests seem to suggest that gatekeeping is reducing the number of potential referrals—most young persons are being diverted to lower tariff disposals and the few still going to custody have a high 'profile' of 'previous' and 'current' offences. Experience (built up by analysing data from the model) shows that these

Figure 4: Information, Policy and Practice model

young people have never been assigned to Alternative to Care and Custody schemes—they are seen by the Courts as 'too serious' to consider alternatives to custody.

The Department then wants to look at the resource options open to them. Should the Alternative to Care and Custody scheme be kept open and, if so, is it likely to slip down-tariff and target at less serious offenders to 'keep the numbers up'. Could the resources be better deployed elsewhere? If the scheme is closed, are the numbers going to custody likely to increase?

These, and other options, are simulated using the model and implications are analysed. A paper is then produced for the Juvenile Justice Strategic Planning Group which agrees to implement the option most consistent with the Group's goals. The evaluation criteria have already been established for each option so the monitoring needs are determined at the same meeting. A close check is to be kept of the changes made and a date for reviewing the change is set.

This may seem somewhat futuristic and hypothetical but I believe the techniques already exist to create such a model. What is required is the *will* and committment to establish the necessary processes.

As a result of the work that we at 'Contract' currently carry out for Durham Social Services and

Probation Departments, we are in the early stages of developing our own dynamic computerised model of the local juvenile justice system. We hope it might evolve as a useful planning tool for systems management and policy development within the County.

I should emphasise that our model is still at a *very* early stage of development so it should be viewed as a 'work in progress', but shows promise as a useful tool for decision-making.

To demonstrate that the Save the Children Fund may have its eye to the future, but has its feet firmly planted in experience, I would like to leave you with an argument raised by Plato about 2,300 years ago. In the Phaedrus he has Socrates tell a story about the Egyptian god Thoth, who explains to the god-king Thamus: 'My lord, I have invented this ingenious thing called writing, and it will improve both the wisdom and the memory of the Egyptians'.

Thamus replies that, on the contrary, writing is an inferior substitute for memory and understanding. He warns: 'Those who acquire it will cease to exercise their memory and become forgetful: they will rely on writing to bring things to their remembrance by external signs instead of on their own internal resources'. They will believe that written words can do more than remind; that words will begin to dictate their actions.[9]

Whether you side with Thoth's optimistic view about writing or tend to agree with Thamus' warnings, experience has shown that both ancients were, to a degree, correct.

As social systems become increasingly complex, mere written statements are inadequate to deal with their complicated inter-relationships. The advent of computerised dynamic modelling may bring with it a re-run of the arguments of Plato's time. 'This ingenious thing called systems modelling will improve both the wisdom and the memory of the juvenile justice policy-makers.' It may, indeed, but only if we remember that wisdom resides in the mind, not the model.

References

1. Feeney, Floyd, "Interdependence as a working concept", in Moxon, D. (ed) opcit.

2. Wesson, A.M., "When is a social inquiry report unneccessary?", *Justice of the Peace*, vol. 150, p. 406.

3. Wesson, A.M., "Recommendations for sentence in probation reports—an argument against", *Justice of the Peace*, vol. 150, p 167.

4. Haggett, Peter, "On Systems and models", in *Systems Behaviour*, Harper and Row, 1981.

5. Morgan, Patricia, "Modelling the Criminal Justice System.", *Home Office Research and Planning Unit Paper 35*, HMSO.

6. Carter, Ruth, et al (1984), *Systems, Management and Change*, London, Harper and Row

7. Pullinger, Hugh, "The Criminal Justice System Model: The Flow Model", *Home Office Research and Planning Unit Paper 36*, HMSO.

8. Moxon, D (ed), *Managing Criminal Justice*, HMSO, 1985.

9. Plato, *Phaedrus and Letters VII and VIII*, Penguin, Harmondsworth, 1973, pp 96-97.

Dynamic Modelling using STELLA™   Barry Hope

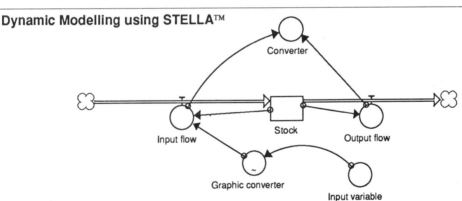

STELLA™ is a dynamic modelling application, written by High Performance Systems Inc., and distributed in the UK by Logoton Ltd. It runs only on the Apple MacIntosh™ range of personal computers. STELLA uses the Macintosh's built-in graphics interface to build 'stock-flow' models from graphical components. These include Stocks, flows and converters.

The model is connected together using links, and the relationship between each part of the system is defined using either mathmatical (or statistical) formulæ, or a graphical representation, which acts as an 'analogue'. Once such a model has been constructed, it can be run in 'real time', the results being output in the form of tables and simple graphs.

Continued...

Figure 1: Stock-flow model of the juvenile justice system to examine the effects of pre-court diversion on the use of custody

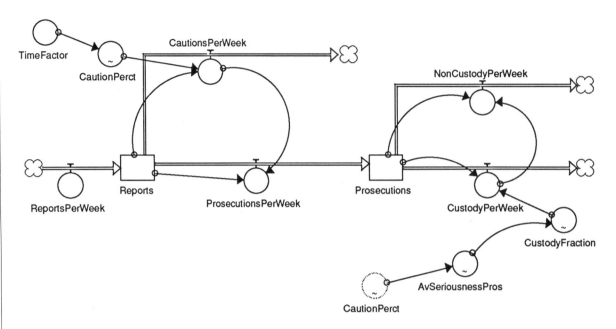

This prototype model uses STELLA™'s graphical features to explore possible relationships between cautioning and custody rates. It is widely recognised that custody rates rise with an increase in pre-court diversion. One reason for this is that as cautions are used to divert increasingly serious offenders from court (in terms of type of offence and antecedent), a higher proportion of those prosecuted will fall within the court's criteria for custody. In addition, it has been suggested that there is a 'backlash' reaction by the courts to an increase in cautioning. This may be caused by the courts responding to what they perceive as an increase in the 'average seriousness' of cases appearing before them. The courts' response to this perceived increase in seriousness would not be in direct proportion to the actual 'average seriousness'. It is likely that there would be a 'threshold of seriousness' above which the custody rate would rise more steeply. The combination of these two factors could result in an overall increase in the numbers being sentenced to custody, however the fall in prosecutions, brought about by an increase in pre-court diversion would off-set the effects of an increased custody rate. The difficulty arises in estimating the aggregate effects of a fall in prosecutions, overlaid with an increase (non-linear) in the proportion of those prosecuted being sent to custody. This model sets out to provide this estimate.

The model

The model (Figure 1) provides a simplified representation of the juvenile justice system. Only the bare essentials have been included. The model could be expanded in various ways to make it more 'realistic', but at the expense of simplicity. There are two basic stocks: **Reports**, fed by **Reports Per Week** at a constant rate of 100 reports per week, which represents the number of young people formally reported by the Police for offences and **Prosecutions**, fed by **Prosecutions Per Week**, a variable rate (governed by the **Cautions Per Week** rate), representing the number of cases being brought before the Court.

Flows out of the system include **Cautions Per Week**, governed by the 'cautioning rate', **Caution Perct**; **Custody Per Week**, governed by the 'custody rate', **Custody Fraction**, and **Non Custody Per Week**. In this case, 'cautioning rate' refers to the proportion of young people diverted from court as a percentage of the total reported, and 'custody rate' refers to the proportion receiving custodial sentences as a percentage of the total number of prosecutions.

Figure 2: Histogram showing hypothetical frequencies of reports of different 'seriousness' of offences

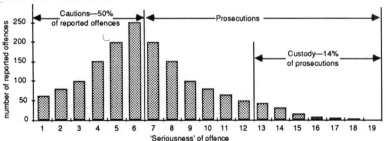

The distribution chosen to represent seriousness of offences is a truncated 'normal' distribution. Offences at the lower end of the scale are likely to be dealt with informally, and would not enter into the formal system.

Inputs

The model is 'driven' by three major inputs. The rise in 'cautioning rate' is provided by a graphical analogue over time, and shows a linear increase in cautioning from 40% to 95% over 35 weeks (see Figure 3). This represents an 'incremental approach' in increasing the use of pre-court diversion. It is possible to use the model to explore the effects of other ways in which the cautioning rate may change. For the sake of simplicity, it is assumed that the cautioning rate is an 'independent variable', ie control of the cautioning rate lies outside the system as represented by this model. In reality, the decisions of a Juvenile Liaison Panel might be affected by what is happening in the courts, but this factor is not under consideration here.

Figure 3: Input analogue showing increase in cautioning rate over time

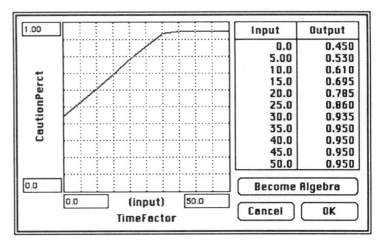

The second input is provided in the form of a graphical relationship between the 'average seriousness' of cases being prosecuted and the cautioning rate (Figure 4). The data used to generate this relationship was provided by the hypothetical frequency distribution shown in Figure 2. It should be explained here that the concept of 'seriousness of case' is not necessarily based on objective or quantifiable factors . Most likely it is an aggregate of several factors, including type of offence, the degree of culpability, antecedent history, values and attitudes of sentencers, and social factors which place the offence in context. As all these factors will combine to influence the Courts' decision whether or not to impose a custodial sentence, they can be represented by one variable. There would be no advantage in attempting to represent all the separate factors which influence sentencing decisions here, as would this would not improve the overall usefulness of the model.

Figure 4: Analogue input showing hypothetical relationship between cautioning rate and average seriousness of cases being prosecuted

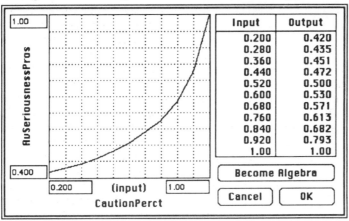

Figure 5: Analogue input showing hypothetical relationship between average seriousness of case and custody rate

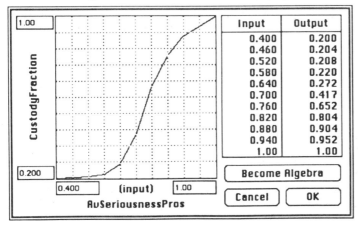

The third input is the factor which represents the 'backlash effect' described earlier. This provides the relationship between the 'average seriousness' and the 'custody fraction' (custody rate). The analogue graph representing this relationship is shown in Figure 5. The assumption here is that the custody rate will not rise in line with an increase in seriousness until a 'threshold' value is reached. After that, the custody rate rises accordingly.

The output from the model is shown here by two graphs. The first, Figure 6, shows the changes in numbers cautioned and sentenced to custody over a 50-week time period. The rise in custodial sentences can be clearly seen, as the courts react to an increase in the 'average seriousness' of cases. This starts to fall again as the reduction in prosecutions takes effect. The relationship between cautions and custodial sentences is shown more clearly by the scatter plot in Figure 7. Here, the rise and fall in the number of custodial sentences can be clearly seen as a function of the cautioning rate.

Figure 6: Output plot showing number of cautions per week and number of custodial sentences per week over time

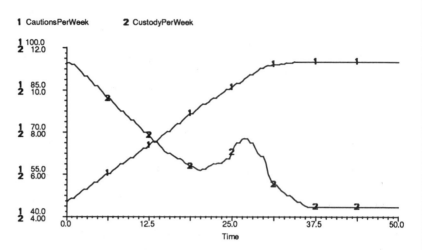

Experimenting with the model
It should be said that this effect only occurs under the circumstances provided by the input variables and specified relationships. By running the model using different sets of input data, the relative importance of the factors identified here can be estimated. For example, when the model is run with a steep increase in the cautioning rate, the 'backlash effect' is more pronounced than when a gradual increase is used. A key factor is the hypothetical relationship between the average 'seriousness' of cases being prosecuted, and the custody rate. A linear relationship between these two variables produces a very different output plot, with the number of custodial sentences falling steadily. Similarly, relatively small changes to the relationship between cautioning rate and average seriousness of cases prosecuted have a major effect on the behaviour of the model. Using a linear relationship here produces an exaggerated 'backlash', which occurs at a lower cautioning rate.

Figure 7: Output scatterplot showing relationship between number of custodial sentences per week and number of cautions per week

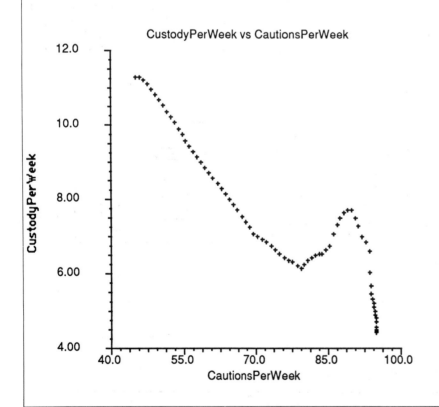

Extending the model
This is a prototype model of one aspect of the juvenile justice system representing a simplified view of the relationship between cautioning and custodial sentencing. It is useful in showing how an increase in pre-court diversion can create effects other than the reduction in prosecution within the system. The model is lacking in an important respect, however, in that feedback loops are absent. These connections between system outcomes and the 'machinery' of the model are most important in the development of sophisticated dynamic models. They produce the forces which maintain a 'dynamic equilibrium' within the system, enabling the model to adapt to changing circumstances. In this case, the connection between outcomes and the model 'machinery' could be provided by allowing for reoffending in the structure of the model, and reflecting the different reconviction rates for cautions, prosecution and custody.

Designing Information Systems

Chris Green is the Information Services Officer for Manchester Probation Service. This paper is an account of the presentation given by him at the Policy and Information Seminar. It has been written by Barry Hope, Training and Development Officer, 'Contract', Save the Children Fund. The paper identifies the ways in which information flows within and between agencies; how such information can be 'trapped' and used to form the basis of a comprehensive juvenile justice monitoring system.

Left to their own devices, juvenile justice agencies tend to develop their own information systems. This happens in an ad hoc way, resulting in a diverse and generally unco-ordinated system of data collection, analysis and dissemination. Often the passage of information within and between agencies reveals more about the policies and practices of these agencies than the nature of crime and offenders. The people within the agencies who know *how* information is collected and transmitted, (but not *why*) are most often the clerical staff.

Information mapping

An aim in developing a co-ordinated information system is to identify information which can be obtained and methods which can be used to 'trap' the information required. A *flowchart* depicting *information flows* can be put together, by studying procedures used by the agency in handling information. This process can take between 6 months and 1 year, and will result in an *information map*, as shown in Figure 1. The most complicated factor in producing the information map is identifying methods of data collection. Figure 1 shows the main methods of data collection and storage associated with Police notification of prosecutions.

Making changes

As a general rule changes to data collection systems are easier to implement at senior management level than at practitioner level (Figure 2). Changes at the 'practice' level involve a greater number of personnel and work places. This can be a limiting factor in determining the scope of changes achievable.

The first step in implementing changes is to determine the type of information required. This task will be simple if related to a clear set of policy objectives. Information systems can be designed in order to produce continuous feedback on the effectiveness of policy, in particular:

a) to provide a measure for the achievement of objectives
   or
b) to identify factors contributing to non-achievement.

At all levels within the agency, it is important to identify the types of information required by practitioners and managers in their day-to-day work, and to base the information system around these needs. For example, the court section may need to keep a

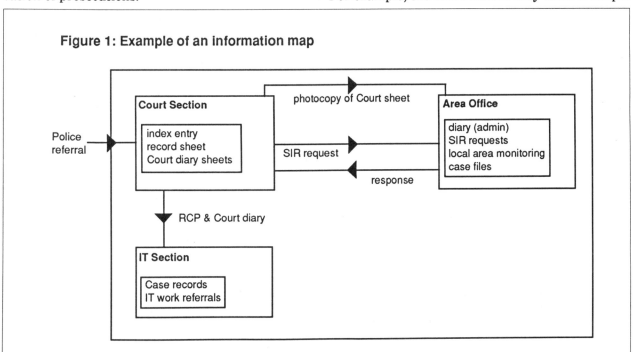

Figure 1: Example of an information map

Police referral → Court Section

Court Section
- index entry
- record sheet
- Court diary sheets

photocopy of Court sheet → Area Office

Area Office
- diary (admin)
- SIR requests
- local area monitoring
- case files

SIR request →
← response

RCP & Court diary ↓

IT Section
- Case records
- IT work referrals

court *diary*, listing cases by date of appearance, and an *index*, listing cases in alphabetical order, and providing details of previous appearances. Field workers will need details of antecedent histories and other client details, for the production of SIRs and other reports.

An information system is only as good as the accuracy of the data collected. Generally, information will only be as accurate as its usefulness to those collecting it.

In addition, the agency may have data needs for external use, for example Home Office / DHSS returns which can be built into the information system.

Once the types of information required have been identified, the 'information map' can be used to identify the sources which can be tapped to provide this data. In the simplest form, this can mean obtaining extra copies of the 'pieces of paper' which flow between and within agencies.

Finally, a time scale needs to be decided on, which strikes a balance between having access to up-to-date information, and allowing time to carry out checks for inaccuracies or uncertainties. In practice, it has been found that the checking process can take up to 17 days.

Collation, analysis and presentation

Once collected, data needs to be collated and analysed. There are three stages to this process, shown in Figure 3.

These are:

1) The establishment of a common case record, a *database* containing client details, and information about charges, reported offences and proceedings.

2) The organisation of data into a *spreadsheet* or 'list' of case records, which enables totals and frequencies to be calculated.

3) The production of tables and diagrams which enable the communications of information in an easily understood form.

Decisions as to how the data will be analysed must be made on the basis of an understanding of criteria for determining the achievement of objectives. Tables produced will provide the measure of success, or point to factors mitigating against the achievement of objectives. Demographic information can be added to 'normalise' information in terms of the relevant changes in local population, particularly important when considering trends.

The collation, analysis and presentation of data on a regular basis should be a routine process within the information system. This process should involve all levels of the agency.

Inter-agency systems

Where common information systems are being used across inter-agency boundaries, it is particularly important that data is collected and classified in the same way. A common 'currency' is crucial to enable joint analysis of data collected by different agencies. Common problems which may need to be overcome are different geographical boundaries used by dif-

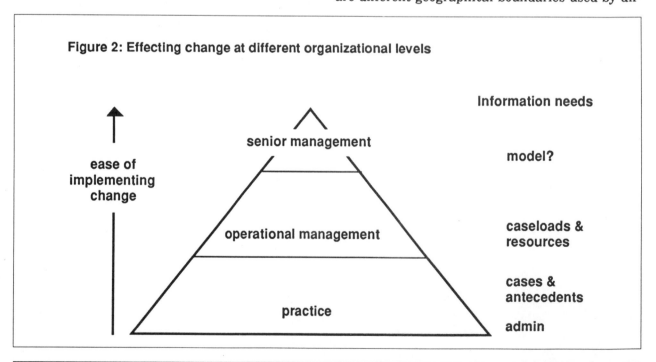

Figure 2: Effecting change at different organizational levels

ferent agencies (eg. social work area, petty sessional division, police sub-division) and time periods used: is a year measured from January to December, April to March or September to August when producing 'annual reports'?

Conclusion

This paper outlines the process by which information systems can be designed and implemented. It provides a framework for information 'mapping' within juvenile justice agencies, and for the collection, analysis and presentation of data on a regular basis. The crucial part of the design process must be in deciding which information is required by the agency. This should, in turn, be determined by the policy objectives of the agency. The aim of an information system should be to provide a measure for the achievement of objectives (or to identify factors leading to non-achievement).

Information is a vital part of the policy-making process. It enables senior managers to plan effectively, allows operational managers to make better use of resources and supplies practitioners with the 'raw materials' for their work. Providing a comprehensive, efficient and accurate information system is a primary task in the management of juvenile justice systems

Figure 3: The collation and analysis of juvenile justice data

sources	contents
1. A common case record (database)	name, identifying information, details of proceedings & charges, etc.
2. Spreadsheet - used to count frequencies	Case records placed in a 'list', ie
3. Tables and diagrams	eg cross-tabulations

name age area court recommendation outcome

No. prev.	SIR Rec	A/D - C/D	Fine	AC	SO
	1				
	2				
	3				
	4				

Current Trends in Criminal Justice Policy

Graham Sutton is a Principal in C1 Division, part of the Criminal Policy Department at the Home Office. In this paper, he outlines current Governmental policy on juvenile offenders, and exercises a little 'crystal-ball gazing' to speculate on policy developments in this field.

A general election can be a time of change. In the run up to the election, the civil service exercises itself in preparing against all possible outcomes based on the content of the various political parties' manifestos. At the Home Office, my colleagues and I had to give thought to the effect a government of a different political colour might have on policy towards young offenders. Possible changes that might prove attractive to a new party in power include; the raising of the age of criminal responsibility; the adoption of the Scottish hearing system in England and Wales; the abolition of custody for juveniles and the foundation of family courts.

On June 12th, the picture became clear. The same party was returned to power, and we have the same Home Secretary. We do have a different Junior Minister with responsibility for criminal policy and crime prevention, John Patten. We do not, however, expect to see significant changes in the broad direction of the Government's criminal policy as it affects young offenders. The Government does not, so far as I am aware, plan to increase the age of criminal responsibility; it does not plan to introduce the Scottish hearings system South of the Border—which is not too far away here; it has yet to make its mind up about a family court (a consultation paper is tentatively proposed for the end of this year); but when it does, I would be surprised to see a family court take on the present juvenile court's responsibility for criminal cases. Nor do I expect to see the establishment of a 'youth court' on the lines proposed by organisations such as ACOP.

There have been a number of important changes in recent years which impinge to a greater or lesser extent on the handling of juvenile offender cases: the introduction of the Crown Prosecution Service, the PACE Act and the advance disclosure of evidence in criminal cases. It is unrealistic to expect any further *radical* change to the system—although DHSS may be bringing forward legislation on care which could have implications for offenders. Changes can be incremental. These are the easiest changes to make, and can be important. What we may see is a 'nibbling away' at the juvenile justice system rather than specific major changes.

Although there has been no change to juvenile justice structures, there has been a very significant change to the context in which young offenders are seen. The emphasis is now very firmly on the inner cities; Mrs. Thatcher lost no time in making this clear. This has important implications for all Home Office policies. We may well be seeing greater emphasis than in the past on inter-departmental approaches to inner city problems. Social policies cannot be compartmentalised if they are to respond effectively to such problems.

Minimum intervention is a key concept in work with juvenile offenders. This is accepted by the Government as an important underlying principle in policy formulation. Most juveniles commit offences during their adolescence (how many of us did not?) and most grow out of it. They need help to grow through that difficult period without being confirmed in their delinquent behaviour. The peak age for offending is 15 for males and 14 for females and 30% of those found guilty or cautioned for indictable offences are aged 10-17. Juveniles are proportionately less involved than adults in crimes of violence. Only 20% of those found guilty or cautioned for offences against the person are juveniles. Offending is a common phenomenon among boys. Self report studies suggest that 90% of young males lapse into some form of crime. Normally, such crime is of a very minor nature, eg smashing windows in empty buildings or riding a bus without paying fare. It is of central importance that our response to delinquent acts does not serve to drive a wayward youngster into becoming a 'career criminal'.

The Government's approach is based on **three diversions:**

- diversion from **crime** (ie crime prevention)
- diversion from **court**
- diversion from **custody**.

Diversion from crime

Increasingly the main thrust of Government's approach to the problem of crime is crime prevention. This will be a central aspect of the Government's work in inner cities. Indeed, there have been a number of important developments in recent years: eg. crime prevention seminars held at Number 10, hosted by the Prime Minister and the Community Programme National Initiative. This initiative does not specifically focus on young offenders, but is concerned with Crime Prevention and the Community at large. The Home Office has established local crime prevention programmes in five areas, one of which is Tyneside. It is gratifying to see a recent reduction in reported offences here in Newcastle.

Another crime prevention related initiative, focussed on schools, is supported through the Educational Support Grant arrangements. One million pounds has been allocated nationally for the support of 'social responsibility' projects. Twenty-two such projects are now in existence in England and Wales. Three of these have been set up in the North East. In Gateshead: £49,300 has been allocated for school pupils to undertake conservation work. In Durham: £23,500 is being provided for the development of social responsibility teaching materials. In Newcastle an allocation of £44,500 has been made for the provision of social, educational and recreational facilities on a housing estate.

The Standing Conference on Crime Prevention has established a Working Group on Juvenile Crime. This group will look specifically at the prevention of juvenile crime and will report to the Standing Conference in November. The main emphasis will be on local responses to meet local problems and the need for a structure involving the effective co-operation of *all* relevant local agencies and concerned individuals. Crime Prevention is a task for the whole community, not just the police. The starting point should be careful study of the local problem (using crime 'profiling' as in the North Tyneside five towns project) enabling targetting of the problem and serving as the focus of action which has the support of the community. There is also a need for careful monitoring and evaluation. The group has also indentified the need for clear and effective leadership which can probably best be provided by the local authority. Local authorities, along with the police, have a central role in juvenile crime prevention since they are responsible for so many relevant services; success will depend upon the personal commitment of senior decision-makers, especially the local authority chief executive. It is especially important to keep up the momentum after the initial enthusiasm has begun to flag and when senior management have reordered their priorities, as they undoubtedly will. The report of the Working Group is unlikely to break much new ground. It will bring together, in a possibly more coherent and focussed way, examples of current thinking and 'good' practice. Of special interest is a youth crime prevention panel which has been established in South Wales. They are about to publish a booklet on how to set up crime prevention schemes in schools. This provides a useful basis for further discussion and action on crime prevention in local areas.

Diversion from court

In the last few years, great emphasis has been placed on the need to keep juveniles out of the formal court system wherever possible, in order to mini-mise the risk of them becoming enmeshed in offending behaviour. Principally, this is done through the use of cautioning by the police. Recent years have seen a considerable increase in cautions administered. We are all familiar with 1985 Circular which provides guidelines for the cautioning of juveniles. Figure 1 shows that there has been some success with 10-16 year olds. This needs to be consolidated, and there is considerable scope for more to be achieved. In 1985 nationally some 39% of 10-13 year old and 22% of 14-16 year old boys were given absolute or conditional discharges. One wonders if there was really a need for all of these young people to be taken to court.

Figure 1: The use of police cautioning in England and Wales		
Age of Offender	1983	1985
10-13	74% (2,900)	79% (3,200)
14-16	42% (7,500)	51% (8,100)
17-20	4% (6,900)	7% (7,200)
source: Home Office		

The Circular did not address the problems of young adults. Is it right that 17-20 year olds should be so far behind in diversion from prosecution? This discrepancy is highlighted if 16 year olds are compared with 17 year olds. In 1985, 36% of 16 year old males dealt with for indictable offences were cautioned; for 17 year olds only 9%. Why is this distinction made? Is there some transfiguring experience at the 17th birthday which makes young people that much more criminally sophisticated? There is increasing awareness, both inside and outside Government, of the need to look at the way young adults are dealt with in the criminal justice system. A great deal has been achieved with juveniles, which must be consolidated. Part of the success with juvenile offenders has been due to the creation of the 'right' climate: people discussing the problems and, in time, all agencies accepting—albeit in some cases reluctantly—the need to respond to them. We must get the dialogue going on the problems faced by young adults.

One of the features of pre-court diversion arrangements for juveniles in some areas has been the creation of Juvenile Liaison Bureaux. Northamptonshire is perhaps the best known example. In 1985, the cautioning rate for juvenile boys was 84%. But even in Northants the cautioning rate for young adult males was only 11%. We are aware that those involved with Juvenile Liaison Bureaux in Northants are beginning to think about extending these arrangements—or something like them—to young adults. Sensibly the bureaux are being cautious. They recognise that different considerations apply to young adults: the local agencies have different responsibilities for young adults than for juveniles, and therefore want to do some research first.

Other projects offer pre-court diversion. The Juvenile Service in Sunderland provides an example of an imaginative way of linking cautioning in with constructive, but voluntary, further action by the community. A similar approach is used by the Sports Counselling project in Southampton. Is there an advantage in this approach, in that the element of compulsion is missing? This is not to endorse these projects as being valuable: I simply draw attention to them.

The greater use of cautioning is, however, not necessarily a universal panacea. Areas of difficulty which arise can include net-widening and difficulties over citation of cautions in Court. Moreover, the wider-scale use of cautioning is not accepted by everybody. Some magistrates in particular feel uneasy about it, and may see it is a kind of 'instant' justice without the safeguards of due process. There may be special concern where cautioning is linked in with—even conditional upon—things such as reparation. In the national debate, we need to heed these concerns and have due regard to them in going forward. Further work is being done within the Home Office to follow up the 1985 cautioning circular. This will include research which will be looking, among other things, at whether the lessons we have learned can be applied to young adults. No doubt we will take on board some of these other areas of concern.

Diversion from custody

The Government is anxious to encourage use of alternatives to custody wherever appropriate. The 1982 Criminal Justice Act provided stronger non-custodial options for the courts, and placed statutory restrictions on the use of custody. CSOs were introduced for 16 year olds and 2,000 such orders were made in 1985. The number of junior attendance centres has increased from 77 in 1979 to 111 now. 10,500 attendance centre orders were made for juveniles in 1985. The Government is now considering increasing the network of senior centres. Coupled with the provision of stronger powers in respect of supervision orders, £18m is being devoted to the development of intensive Intermediate Treatment facilities under the DHSS initiative (LAC(83)3). Important claims have been made for the success of this initiative in keeping juveniles out of care and custody. It seems likely that these schemes have had some impact on custodial sentencing, as there has been a significant drop in use of custody in the last few years for juveniles. In 1986 about 4,400 juveniles received custodial sentences. This compares with 6,000 in 1985 and about 7,800 in 1981, the peak year. The situation is less encouraging for young adults. 1985 was the peak year with 25,300 17-20 year olds being given custodial sentences. This figure was reduced to 21,300 in 1986. There is a need to consolidate achievements with juveniles, and to build on the lessons we have learned with them to find ways in which the custody rate for young adults can be reduced. Some voluntary organisations are already thinking about introducing intensive IT schemes for young adults. It has also been suggested that what is needed is a new sentence for young adults, perhaps something not yet tried with juveniles. It is frequently the case that all options have been exhausted for juveniles, leaving the courts with no other option but custody for young adults. We also need to develop a consistent approach. There are often wide variations in the custody rates of courts in the same area and between different parts of the country. This has been called 'justice by geography'. Why does it happen? What can be done about it? One way is to draw courts' attention to their own and adjoining courts' figures.

Criminal Justice Bill

Before finishing, it is perhaps worthwhile to consider the young offender provisions in the Criminal Justice Bill.

The Bill contains very little reference to young offenders, but no doubt attempts will be made to amend it. The main provisions of this Bill are as follows:

- The strengthening of statutory restrictions on custodial disposals.
- Increased sanctions for breach of supervision orders imposed as alternatives to custody.
- The re-introduction of powers to attach school attendance requirements to supervision orders.
- The introduction of powers for the Secretary of State to hold those with short youth custody sentences in detention centres.

It is important to stress that the stronger sanctions available for the breach of supervision orders will not apply in the case of the breach of a school attendance condition.

In addition to these proposals, active consideration is being given to the introduction of a single custodial sentence to replace youth custody and detention centre orders, as indicated by Lord Caithness in the second reading of the Bill. Provision for a single custodial sentence for young offenders was introduced during the committee stage of the Bill in the House of Lords. Another important amendment affecting young offenders was the introduction of a provision for time spent in secure accommodation during a remand in care to count towards an eventual custodial sentence.

Conclusion

The general framework which has been established since 1982 for dealing with juvenile offenders has enabled further progress to be made in diverting juvenile offenders from the criminal justice system and from custody. The growth in the use of cautioning, the activities of a number of juvenile bureaux, the success of so many intermediate treatment projects and the growing use of the community service order for sixteen year olds all offer hope for a further reduction. We need to consolidate the successes we have had with juveniles; they have been too hard-earned to let them go. But we must at the same time apply the lessons we have learned to work with young adults. Not blindly, but by making the necessary adjustments to take account of the differing circumstances of this important age group.

Bibliography

ARMSTRONG, R. H. R. and HOBSON, M (1972): *"The Use of Games in Planning"*, **Long Range Planning**, Vol. 5. No.1. pp 62-66.

BARTON, A. (1984): **The Criminal Justice System Model, the Police Sub-model** (Publication 39/84), Home Office Scientific Research and Development Branch.

BAUER, Raymond and GERGEN, Kenneth (Eds) (1968): **The Study of Policy Formulation**, Free Press.

BREHNY, Michael and HALL, Peter (1987): *"The Strange Death of Strategic Planning and the Victory of the Know-Nothing School"*, **Built Environment**, Vol. 10, No.2. pp 95-99.

BURROWS, B. C. (1986): *"Planning, Information Technology and the Post-Industrial Society"*, **Long Range Planning**, Vol. 19, No.2. pp 79-89.

BUTLER, Sid (1982): *"Mathematical Modelling of the Criminal Justice System"*, **Home Office Research Bulletin**, No.14.

CARLEY, Michael (1980): **Rational Techniques in Policy Analysis (Policy Studies Institute)**, Heinemann Educational Books.

CARTER, Ruther, et al (1984): **Systems, Management and Change (a graphic guide)**, London, Harper & Row/ OUP.

CHECKLAND, Peter (1981): **Systems thinking, systems practice**, London, Wiley.

COOPER, Joan (Chair) (1987): **Time for Change—a new framework for dealing with juvenile crime and offenders**, NACRO.

CUSHMAN, Robert C. (1980): **Criminal Justice Planning for Local Governments**, United States Department of Justice.

de SMIT, J. and RADE, N. (1980): *"Rational and Non-Rational Planning"*, **Long Range Planning**, April 1980, pp 87-101.

DECKER, Scott H. (Ed) (1984): **Juvenile Justice Policy: analysing trends and outcomes**, Sage Publications.

DENNING, Basil W. (1971): **Corporate Planning, Selected Concepts**, Longon, McGraw-Hill.

DROR, Yehezkel (1973): **Public Policy Making Re-examined**, Leonard Hill Books.

EDWARDS, Helen (1987): *"Policy Directions for Juvenile Crime"*, Speech Given to the JCS Leicester Conference, May 1987, Juvenile Crime Section, NACRO.

FALK, Nicholas and LEE, James (1978): **Planning the Social services**, Saxon House.

FALKIN, Gregory (1979): **Reducing Delinquency—A Strategic Planning Aproach**, U.S., D.C. Heath & Co

FALUDI, Andreas (ed) (1973): **A Reader in Planning Theory**, Oxford, Pergammon Press.

FOX, James (1981): **Models in Quantitative Criminology**, Academic Press.

GREGG, Phillip, (Ed) (1976): **Problems of Theory in Policy Analysis**, Lexington Books.

HAGGETT, PETER (1981): *"On Systems and Models"*, in **Systems Behaviour**, Harper and Row.

HAMBLETON, Robin (1978): **Policy Planning and Local Government**, Hutchinson.

HAMBLETON, Robin (1986): **Rethinking Policy Planning, a Study of Planning Systems Linking Central and Local Government**, School of Advanced Urban Studies, Bristol University.

HAYES, Robert (1985): *"Strategic Planning - forward in reverse? Are corporate planners going about things the wrong way round?"*, **Harvard Business Review**, November-December 1986 pp 11-119

HOLLIS, Guy, Coopers and Lybrand (1986): *"Strategic Management—obstacles to implementation"*, **Public Finance and Accountancy**, 21 November 1986, pp 12-14.

HONEY, M. (1979): *"Corporate Planning and the Chief Executive"*, **Local Government Studies**, September, 1979.

JUVENILE OFFENDERS TEAM, (1985): **Monitoring Community Alternatives to Custody and Care**, NACRO.

KAHN, Alfred J. (1969): **Studies in Social Policy and Planning**, New York, Russell Sage Foundation (Esp. Ch. III *"Children in Trouble: problem-focussed planning on the local level"*).

KAHN, Alfred J. (1969): **Theory and Practice of Social Planning**, New York, Russell Sage Foundation (Esp. Ch. 5 *"Formulation of Policy, the Standing Plan"*).

KOBERG, Don and BAGNALL, Jim (1981): **The Revised All-new Universal Traveller: A soft-systems guide to creativity, problem solving and the process of reaching goals**, Kaufmann.

LOCKE, Trevor (1982): *"The Range of Strategic and Practical Options in work with Young People in Trouble"* (background paper for a group discussion at the CVS Conference, Bath, Sept. 1982), National Youth Bureau.

LOCKE, Trevor (1982): **Planning—strategic and practical options in work with young people in trouble**, Scottish IT Resource Centre.

LOCKE, Trevor (1987): *"Policy and Planning in Juvenile Justice"* (Notes of a seminar given at the National Intermediate Treatment Federation Conference, September 1987), NACRO.

LOCKE, Trevor (March 1987): *"Juvenile Justice Policy, Theory and Concepts"*, Notes for Seminar Paticipants, Juvenile Crime Section, NACRO.

LONDON, Keith (1976): **The People Side of Systems**, London, McGraw Hill.

MIER, Robert et al (1986): *"Strategic Planning and the Pursuit of Reform, Economic Development and Equity"*, **APA Journal**, Summer 1986, pp 299-309.

MILHAM, Spencer et al (1987): *"Strategies emerge and policies drift"*, **Social Services Insight**, April 10, 1987, pp 19-21.

MOORE, Keith and FREEMAN, Isobel (1986): *"Poverty and Planning—how technology can help"*, **Social Services Insight**, December 5, 1986, pp 12-19.

MORGAN, P. (1987): **Modelling the Criminal Justice System**, (HORU Paper 53), Home Office Research and Planning Unit.

MOXON, David (Ed) (1985): **Managing Criminal Justice, a collection of papers**, Home Office Research and Planning Unit, HMSO.

MURRAY, Nicholas (1987): *"Rethinking Public Services"*, **Social Services Insight**, July 24, 1987, pp 8 - 9.

MURRAY, Peter and LETCH, Roger (1987): **Getting Closer to the Public**, Luton, Local Government Training Board.

NAGEL, Stuart (Ed.) (1977): **Modelling the Criminal Justice System**, U.S. Sage Publications.

PARKER, Chris and ALCOE, Jan (1986): *"Dinosaur Strategies"*, **Social Services Insight**, October 4 - October 11, 1986, pp 22-23.

PARKER, Chris and ALCOE, Jan (1986): *"Implementing the Ideal"*, **Social Services Insight**, October 31, 1986, pp 21-22.

PULLINGER, Hugh (1985): **The Criminal Justice System Model, the Flow Model**, (HORU Paper 36), Home Office Research and Planning Unit.

RICE, Susan (1984): **The Criminal Justice System Model: Magistrates Courts Sub-Model** (HORU Paper 24) Home Office Research and Planning Unit.

RITCHIE, Ian (undated): **Organisation Development and Working in a Juvenile Justice System**, London, NACRO.

TSICHRITZIS, and LOCHOVSKY, F. (1982): **Data Models**, Prentice Hall.

VINCENT, Dr. Jacky (1980): **Planning Resources for Community-based Treatment of Juvenile Offenders (Final Report)**, London, Social Policy Research.

WILDAVSKI, Aaron (1980): **The Art and Craft of Policy Analysis**, U.K., MacMillan.

WESSON, A.M.(1986): *"When is a social inquiry report unneccessary?"*, **Justice of the Peace**, vol. 150, p. 406.

WESSON, A.M.(1986): *"Recommendations for sentence in probation reports—an argument against"*, **Justice of the Peace**, vol. 150, p. 167.